Twin Sons
of
Different
Mirrors

POEMS IN DIALOGUE

Twin Sons
of
Different
Mirrors

Jack Driscoll/Bill Meissner

Photographs by Nancy Campbell

MILKWEED EDITIONS

TWIN SONS OF DIFFERENT MIRRORS

Printed in the United States of America.
Published in 1989 by *Milkweed Editions*.
Post Office Box 3226
Minneapolis, Minnesota 55403

Books may be ordered from the above address.

92 91 90 89   4 3 2 1

Milkweed Editions gratefully acknowledges the funding support of the Jerome
Foundation, the First Bank System Foundation, the Dayton Hudson Foundation
for Dayton's and Target Stores, United Arts (through the Arts Development
Fund), the Literature Program of the National Endowment for the Arts, and the
generosity of individual donors.

Library of Congress Cataloging-in-Publication Data

Driscoll, Jack, 1946—
    Twin sons of different mirrors.

    I. Meissner, Bill, 1948-   . II. Title.
PS3554.R496T86 1989   811'.54   89-3106
ISBN 0-915943-35-2 (pbk.)

The authors gratefully acknowledge the magazines and journals in which these
poems first appeared: *Chelsea:* "The Somnambulist's Music"; *Milkweed Chronicle:*
"The Sailor," "Test Drive: Death Of The Mechanic," "Why He Never Wears
Shoes," "The Pause," "Looking Glass," "Leaving The Hometown," "After The
Storm, He Lifts His Head From The Pillow," "The Catcher's Last Game," "Walk-
ing Into The Dream"; *Northwest Review:* "Part Of The Waking," "Keeping In
Touch," "First Kiss"; *The Paper:* "A Story Of Hunger And Thirst"; *Passages
North:* "Winter Fishing", "Returning Only Part Way Home".

Dedicated to the U.S. Postal Service

≈

"Mail, over any length of time,
will tell secrets a neighbor could not guess."
Charles Olson
The Post Office

Foreword

Before reading *Twin Sons of Different Mirrors* I wondered about what I'd find. My first, and final, questions concerned the poems themselves. What would collaboration produce? I knew Jack Driscoll, and his poetry, but did not know Bill Meissner's work. Working together, co-laboring, what would these two poets make? What shape would the poems take? Would they be short or long, private or public, conventional or not? What would they see and say about the world, about the poets, about poetry?

These are questions we always have, voiced or not, every time we approach a book of poems. In this case, the questions were magnified by knowing the unique method of composition.

Other questions were more directly about *process*. Poems are not only artifacts; they are the imaginative creation of those artifacts as well. From a letter by Jack Driscoll, I knew that the poems were written "two lines at a time between me and Bill; I'd write two and he'd respond with two of his own, back and forth that way until the poem was finished. Then changes recommended back and forth, after the poem seemed 'first draft' ready, though strangely, they underwent much less revision than my own poems usually demand." Though the mystery of accommodating another imagination, vision, and voice remained, Jack's account gave me a sense of logistics. I also learned that the book, "Dedicated to the U.S. Postal Service," took ten years to write — a long but not surprising length of time. There was no knowing, however, who began individual poems, who ended them, who gave them titles, who wrote what lines. In short, I wouldn't know where the borders were between Bill Meissner and Jack Driscoll.

And why should I? Such merging and obscuring of the individual poets' voices would emphasize the invented voice and would take collaboration to its full and natural extension. It is possible, certainly, to write poems back and forth (and forward at the same time, toward the unity a good book will have) without ever giving up individual creation of poems. The result is dialogue. Although dialogue is possible in poetry, and even in the individual poem, the important arguments are with ourselves, as Yeats, a poet nevertheless fond of dialogue, observed. A whole book of poems marked by voices alternating every two lines would sound schizophrenic at worst, and at best would probably lack coherence. Going in, I wondered whether I'd find two dictions, two syntaxes, two fields of imagery, emotion, thought.

I'm glad to report that in *Twin Sons of Different Mirrors* Meissner and Driscoll have avoided the problems possible in collaboration. The arguments here *are* internal, or seem so. Together, the poets speak with a single, unified voice, much like identical twins who complete one another's sentences. And one of the principal rewards of this collaboration is that the voice — informed by two histories, two visions, two imaginations — is very vigorous. Nowhere do the poems slip into a rut; they literally "take turns," turns that keep the language, and the listener, alert.

Perhaps related to. the method — lines coming out of preceding lines but also out of nowhere (or at least from another state!) — is the dominant motif of *Twin Sons*. Everywhere in the book we find a tension between sleep and waking, between the inner and outer life. The images from another's consciousness must seem much like those from our own unconscious, images that dreaming so often offers up. Everywhere I was aware (because I was looking?) of self and other, of the interpenetration of life and life. In "The Visitor" Meissner/Driscoll writes: "I hear him singing in another language," someone who has arrived with "no tracks, no snowshoes leaning / against the door."

Song is an appropriate metaphor; this book is two-part harmony. The poetic communion of *Twin Sons of Different Mirrors* becomes finally more than method, becomes, in fact, the book's aim and main achievement, the seamless singing of two talents to us. "A line will take us hours maybe," wrote Yeats, "Yet if it does not seem a moment's thought, / Our stitching and unstitching has been naught." Over time and distance, Jack Driscoll and Bill Meissner have done the imaginative work that makes poetry, and makes it beautiful to our ears.

—Michael Pettit

TWIN SONS OF DIFFERENT MIRRORS

≈

≈
Keeping
in Touch

Keeping In Touch

Even if no one ever asks me
to talk about wheels
I will live knowing they watch
the spokes in my mouth
and I will pretend to sing
like a bicycle in the attic.

I will write letters to my friends
explaining nothing,
and they will reply with empty envelopes
that float to my door like milkweed.
I will phone them, long-distance,
and remain silent, letting them guess
whose voice is the stalled engine
on the other end. Before they hang up

I will pour water into the phone
and listen to the sound of them rusting.

A Story Of Hunger And Thirst

I have let my fingers turn to glass.
For too many weeks they kept
scratching sleep from the white sheets.
Now, when I touch my face,
it blurs, like milk spilled across a table.
I imagine myself sitting down for a meal
at an all night diner,
the waitress lifting a white mug of coffee.
Instead, I am walking along roadsides in darkness,
the empty cornfields swallowing the few flakes of snow
that float in front of my lips.

First Kiss

When he first discovered his dentures
in the garden, he put them
in a glass of cut flowers, watched them
sprout water lilies between the teeth.
Each flower frightened his wife like
a snake asleep in her clay pot.
When he smiled, his gums
were pale roses pressed for years
against the fishbowl of her dreams.
It was always that way between them,
the soft bites underwater, the kisses
that leave a taste for decades in their mouths.

How My Father Explained The World

My father said madness was like ice,
it was what we all lived by.
Those days we pushed hard on accelerators,
the chained tires cutting huge figure-eights
on the frozen lake.
We never heard the cracking, the pistol fire
beneath us. Father said ice was like love,
something we never understood on our tongues
as we tried to surface
from beneath a body of water that held us
with invisible arms, trying not to hurt us,
squeezing as hard as it could.

Shopping At
Woolworth's Five And Dime

It is halloween and so many masks stare up
from the store counters.
They're like pies I should put my face into,
like wheels spinning a witch's curse,
the eye holes deep as caves
I can climb into and stay
for months, living only on seeds or insects.
No one would know it was me
looking out through the window after closing,
me longing for some child's face
on the other side of the thick plate glass.

After The Storm,
He Lifts His Head From The Pillow

The bird in the yard
is all that's left
in his memory.
Once the hailstorm hit,
his life was scattered across the countryside,
the wreckage of so much ice.

The clouds gone, he can walk outside
and lift the wing, its feathers
white and floating from his hands.

Days The Hobos Returned

When I kneel, I find
all the buckets have been stolen.
The well is swallowing hard
against the black sky,
though water is nothing more than
a few stars caught in a throat.

There is an echo
in my ear;
it speaks of an empty mine shaft
where two old men
still huddle together waiting,
looking up, feeding a small fire
between them with wet wood.

Looking Glass

In the dark shell of a lightbulb
he saw his face again —
the useless eyes staring,
open to whatever breeze passes
through glass. She moved in
and out of his life, her skirt
dropped on the ground, her lips
bending to him like grass:

the taste was
something like a cool stream
he had known once,
the mirror of it cracking
his forehead to a thousand pieces.

Building The New House

How many times I have stood in this
attic, watching the cracks
filling with light, the air my lungs have let go.
How many times I have cried,
              the pain of hornets flying toward
              the center of my eyes.
They nest in my skull. Even now
I can feel them
              chewing their soft mud,
              building this colony I speak to
              with words that sting and sting.

≈

Disguises
That
Fool
No One

The Watch

Broken. It was always broken when he
picked it up:
        spring twisted, the second hand
        bent back to a night
        that refused to end,
        the calendar blackening on his desk.
        Before bed he would wind and wind
as if waking were only the
ticking of his heart.
        But the hands were still,
        flattened black snakes
        exploding like silent alarms
that kept pointing and pointing at him,
waking him from the dead.

Investments

He carries the briefcase full of water
into an open field
and empties it there, drop by
drop, like a rain
straining to be seen,
the sun counting the seconds
until it evaporates. The man
walking there is thirsty, the roots in his throat
stretching like dollar bills
pulled taut between his thumbs.
Too old for drinking,
he stoops to the earth, his palms
dry as old banknotes
he has planted each spring under a full moon.

Why He Never Wears Shoes

The reason he was always waking,
he told her, was to taste the grass
on his bare feet. She should have known
exactly what he meant. He remembered the night
she stood naked near a line of trees,
whispered into the green of his ear:
>how much I love
>the fragile tips of your toes, the way they never
>take root.

He said: I love your
>clay, your riverbanks
>impacted with smooth bones.

>These feet have sung to them, these feet running
and running without ever lifting from the ground.

Taxidermist

I have always wanted to be a taxidermist—
the thin blood of wood ducks
could thicken my own.
Late at night you would find me, huddled
under a kerosene lamp,
the black marble eyes of a bear or coyote
rolling on my desk.
I know they see the stars through the drawn shades,
their matted fur rising in a wind
though all the windows are locked,
though the door is bolted tight
like a bullet in a rifle.

The Sailor

Twice in his life
he began to explain all
the tatters in his skin.

The first time
he rolled up his sleeve
he gasped at the thin bones,
the trickle of veins that smiled weakly at him.

The second time, standing
in shorts, he saw the mirror blur,
his knees rock back and forth
like the ribs of wooden boats
swaying at the bottom of the sea.

Test Drive:
Death Of The Mechanic

I step on the accelerator,
slide around the final curve,
the shoulder so soft
it could be the pillow where
I rested my head as a child, dreamed
of pulling out at 80 miles an hour
to pass the neighborhood kids
on tricycles. I pretended
the dust in their eyes came from years of speeding
through small towns, leaving the main streets,
sliding into the funnels of themselves.

As the car rolls over I remember
how I'd wake from sleep,
my hands holding the dark in front of me
like a locked steering wheel.

Salesman's Resumé
Of Disasters

I always put my foot into the wrong pantleg,
find the zipper behind me
pulled open like a broken screen
through which I crawl, my cheeks
tattooed with permanent press stitches, scars
I must wear the rest of my life.

When I look into the sleeves of my Arrow shirts,
moths come out of storage
to chew the frail patches
of my eyelids.

At last I slide on my dull business shoes,
those two black explosions that will carry me
to every small shop, newsstand, office
with bosses smiling at my confused lips, my tie
turned inside out like a tongue
that does nothing but lie.

The Visitor

There are no tracks, no snowshoes leaning
against the door. But someone has already arrived.
I hear him turning the faucet in the sink,
lifting my razor, slowly
the way morning lifts behind the sharp edge of the roof.
I hear him singing in another language:
Gaelic, or German, I'm not certain.
And the splashing water answers him,
the steam of the shower like a cloud he can hide in.
Even when I enter he stands next to me,
rolling the soap in his palms,
every inch of tile washing smooth
like clean skin.

The Grocer's Dream

All he can think about are gardens,
whole fields of vegetables swarming,
ripening after dark. Each time he wakes
another melon has grown
huge as a dream. In the mirror
he thinks he could pick
his swollen ears, his eyeballs,
place them carefully
in perfect rows on the plastic counter.
Housewives, hungry for bargains,
will barge into the room,
fill their fragile arms with the bulk
of him, go running toward their daughters,
saying look, finally a man whose feet
hold to the earth like two giant taproots.

The Catcher's Last Game

Even when he turns from the diamond,
he cannot shake the pain from his wrist,
the ball so heavy it pulls his shoulder to the
ground. Everywhere, the dust of his past
spins like the first headache of his life.

He swings the bat once more and can't remember
his name, the score, the face of the man
coming down the line from third
as they all gather around him, a circle closing
like a catcher's mask he can never take off.

≈
Fishing
For Our
Lives

The Somnambulist's Music

I have tried to walk across the lake
a dozen times, the ice
so thin I could be swimming on my feet.
Beneath, the fish looked up
at the small, dark lagoons
of my soles. I could hear
the moon, my ear a wave carrying
all the songs fish lips have longed
to sing. The first note
is a stone sinking for years.

The Pause

These fish on the bank,
gutted, don't know
the weight of deep water,
where mud swirls from the bottom
of a deep lake like grief
they will no longer have to pull
through their gills.
Their insides are pink, their eyes dreaming of
absence, the hollow tunnel they might swim through,
the way their entrails dream
of swimming upstream
after being washed from their·bellies.

The Lure

When he first netted the catfish
he saw it was his mother,
dark whiskers
coming toward his face gasping,
the hook in her blue lips
shimmering like a jewel
she was about to swallow.

He wanted to kiss her
the way his father once did,
pulling her close in a boat,
his tongue like a lure
she could not resist.

Winter Fishing

It was my first shanty.
No wonder I left off the roof
and built a floor of nails.
When I looked up at night,
the stars were schooled like fish.
I thought, this is what it must be like
to be adrift at sea,
to be a carpenter, an apron full of hooks.

I imagined the sky freezing like a huge pond,
something so deep I could lower a line forever
toward those open mouths.
Perhaps this is the way all fishing begins
or ends, the moon swimming by like a lure,
and me, tugging this line of light, pulling it closer.

The Migration

All the salmon keep turning back,
their own shadows waving from the sandy bottom.
They return toward the pull of blue
somewhere deep inside the brain.
Their fins flicker like lightning,
like the fire of birth
they struggle toward, abandoning the current.
Far downriver, they glide past the hooks,
their soft mouths opening wide on the whole ocean
as though they could swallow even themselves.

Rising
and
Falling
Toward
Sleep

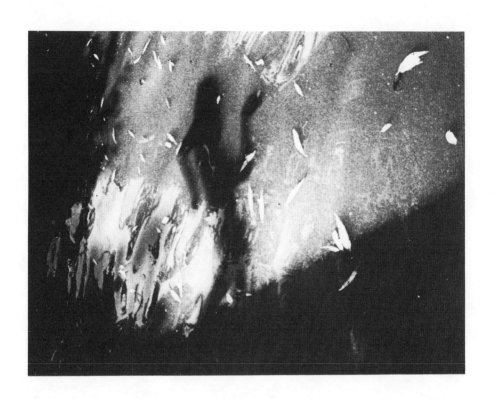

The Rising

At any time
you should be able to open your hands
and let go of the broken glass
as if it were nothing more
than dry birds' beaks
or the ice spit from a woman's mouth.

You sit here, night after night.
The windows behind you leap up
like flat, transparent fish
you are afraid to look through.
When the lake crawls under the trees,
washing the roots, everything you own
turns shades of white or
black, everything
is snow or coal dust. In dreams
your chest fills with water, a sifting
of stone, a rise and fall inside you.

Something Like Waking

The crows keep flying backwards across the field.
I lie down, pull the undersides of feathers
slowly to my eyes.
                              When I wake,
the crows are gone,
but the sky is so full of silence,
a blackness passing like wings
in front of the sun.

Ceilings

Nothing I can do will change the way
the roof keeps wanting to lift above my head,
keeps straining from the instant I fall asleep.
Not a night goes by
without me climbing from bed,
dropping the swirl of covers below me like clouds.

Naked, I stand and stare at the timbers
creaking, the nails pulling out.
They drop into my palm,
tiny canes that have tapped the edges of rivers,
the deep ravines, the hollow, empty rooms of my face.

Reading Before Sleep

The insects crawl from page to blank page
surprising me with their tinfoil legs.
They come without wings
like the parts of letters
inside silver attic boxes
that have not crumbled to white ash.

I turn the book over,
its spine bending
like the hill of my spine bends
when it feels the weight
of water, dark and deep
in a coal mine spring, a season
without legs or fins

that swims up close to the eyes
the instant before sleep.

Part Of The Waking

In the morning, even before
the dog is awake,
I have put on all
my dreaming clothes and walked outside
across the lawn with my shoes
in my hand.
But this will not be enough.
The touch of the grass will taste like green teeth,
and the hammock, stretched between the unpruned apple trees,
can barely hold the day's weight. I must keep saying to myself,
lean back, back far enough until you can see
the apples fade from red to pale blue
and feel the ground underneath inhaling,
pulling through the squares of rope
one by one like pieces of sleep.

Cavities

There is a sound so deep in my ear
I can almost hear it
uncoiling like a thin black wire
through my thirtieth year. I listen
all night to the junked car, the
hollow center of the watch spring,
whatever metallic whisper
collapses on my tongue.
In the morning, my face in the mirror
has changed seasons:
my one gold tooth
a sun sleeping all winter in the snowbank
of my mouth.

Almost Ready For Sleep

My dresser drawers are filled with lightbulbs.
I think she hid them there,
thin grey skulls. I shake one,
and the room darkens
like the center of a candle.
She's already asleep, waiting for me.
In the mirror my smile glows like a filament
no switch can extinguish.

Walking Into The Dream

The first thing I think, as I lift my foot
from the ground, is the weight
pressing under my tongue. Each step
forces
another taste of shoe leather wearing thin
down the throat's dark trail. I open my mouth
filling with snow. I cannot hear
the voices of bears calling
from a region so deep
no wind has ever bothered with words.

≈

Returning
Only
Part Way
Home

The Chase

Some nights I drive the Chevy without lights;
I come to the curve, turn the wheel
the way my father turned in his sleep
after a drive across the long landscape,
those miles he believed he could cover
before anyone woke in the morning.
I'd follow him,
tailing him into the darkness, always keeping
the same sure distance,
sparks rising from his tail pipe
as he tried so often to lose me.

Running Away From Home

This is the hallway of childhood.
I stroll it slowly, noticing the crayon marks
on the wall, the open window,
white curtains blowing towards me like hair.
There is a door without knobs
and someone keeps knocking to get in or out.
I lean against it, imagining the voice of the stars.
the full moon that looked so much like my face
the night before I was born.

Graduation

As I wake, the football spirals
toward me, a white light, really,
the tail end of that same dream.
I've had since high school.
I climb out of bed, suddenly older,
and lace up the high, black cleats.
Under the moon I go deep, angling
across the front lawn,
looking up for that last long pass,
my arms still cradling the emptiness.

Reruns

The night the television set went dark,
he turned toward the window, his face starving
like a winter moon. The shadows
became small animals crawling back to the woods
where he sat with his .22,
his trigger finger smoothing the metal blue.
The whole sky was a blank screen that night
as he piled snow up to his waist,
and thought of wolves on his scent,
their grey eyes full of static,
seeing him wherever they turned,
seeing him like the one man in the movie
they were always unable to kill.

Leaving The Hometown

I fill the gas tank with snow
and begin driving
into what I thought was a blizzard.
Instead it is sand, swirling
across the road, stinging my face.

I swing my wheels into a curve,
a memory of falling. There is a cliff
where I tiptoed once, my pockets
filled with stones
that I dropped over the edge.

I listened to them
clinking like spark plugs
against the rocks. Behind me
the car was stalled, my suitcase open
on the back seat, a parachute
billowing out like exhaust.

Returning Only Part Way Home

I turn through sleep,
my wings buoying me high above the landscape.
There's my father smoking a cigarette alone
on the front porch, my mother in the back.
She is worried again, calling and calling,
her voice soft as a net.
Now they both shine flashlights
up through the openings of trees.
What they see are only the beams evaporating
into the darkness, so thin and fragile
no one would ever dare climb down.

Making Room

Maybe it's the wind
that breaks its own back

then slides into the nearest mailbox
with its first few flakes of snow.

When I hear that sudden song
I turn toward windows, allowing myself room
to throw off my clothes, to dance naked
in the echo of myself

allowing the wind room
to lift all my unused pages
and carry them away.

≈ ≈

Jack Driscoll writes and fishes in northern Michigan. His poems have appeared in many national magazines including *Poetry, Antaeus, The Ohio Review, Michigan Quarterly Review*, and *Poetry Northwest*. Winner of the 1988 PEN/Nelson Algren Fiction Award, Driscoll's stories have appeared regularly in magazines and newspapers including *The Georgia Review, Indiana Review and Witness*. His three collections of poetry are *The Language of Bone, Fishing The Backwash*, and *Building The Cold From Memory*.

Bill Meissner grew up in Iowa and Wisconsin. He attended the University of Wisconsin — Stevens Point where he received a B.S. degree in English. He attended the University of Massachusetts to complete his M.A. He and Jack Driscoll met in Massachusetts and shortly after their graduation they began work on their collaborative poems through the mail. Meissner coordinates the Creative Writing Program at St. Cloud State University, and has won numerous awards for his poetry which has been collected in two books: *Learning To Breathe Underwater* and *The Sleepwalker's Son*, both published by Ohio University Press. He lives with his wife and son in St. Cloud, Minnesota.

≈ ≈ ≈ ≈ ≈ ≈ ≈ ≈ ≈ ≈ ≈ ≈ ≈ ≈ ≈ ≈
≈ ≈ ≈ ≈ ≈ ≈ ≈ ≈ ≈ ≈ ≈ ≈ ≈ ≈ ≈ ≈
≈ ≈ ≈ ≈ ≈ ≈ ≈ ≈ ≈ ≈ ≈ ≈ ≈ ≈ ≈ ≈
≈ ≈ ≈ ≈ ≈ ≈ ≈ ≈ ≈ ≈ ≈ ≈ ≈ ≈ ≈ ≈
≈ ≈ ≈ ≈ ≈ ≈ ≈ ≈ ≈ ≈ ≈ ≈ ≈ ≈ ≈ ≈
≈ ≈ ≈ ≈ ≈ ≈ ≈ ≈ ≈ ≈ ≈ ≈ ≈ ≈ ≈ ≈
≈ ≈ ≈ ≈ ≈ ≈ ≈ ≈ ≈ ≈ ≈ ≈ ≈ ≈ ≈ ≈
≈ ≈ ≈ ≈ ≈ ≈ ≈ ≈ ≈ ≈ ≈ ≈ ≈ ≈ ≈ ≈
≈ ≈ ≈ ≈ ≈ ≈ ≈ ≈ ≈ ≈ ≈ ≈ ≈ ≈ ≈ ≈
≈ ≈ ≈ ≈ ≈ ≈ ≈ ≈ ≈ ≈ ≈ ≈ ≈ ≈ ≈ ≈
≈ ≈ ≈ ≈ ≈ ≈ ≈ ≈ ≈ ≈ ≈ ≈ ≈ ≈ ≈ ≈
≈ ≈ ≈ ≈ ≈ ≈ ≈ ≈ ≈ ≈ ≈ ≈ ≈ ≈ ≈ ≈
≈ ≈ ≈ ≈ ≈ ≈ ≈ ≈ ≈ ≈ ≈ ≈ ≈ ≈ ≈ ≈
≈ ≈ ≈ ≈ ≈ ≈ ≈ ≈ ≈ ≈ ≈ ≈ ≈ ≈ ≈ ≈
≈ ≈ ≈ ≈ ≈ ≈ ≈ ≈ ≈ ≈ ≈ ≈ ≈ ≈ ≈ ≈
≈ ≈ ≈ ≈ ≈ ≈ ≈ ≈ ≈ ≈ ≈ ≈ ≈ ≈ ≈ ≈
≈ ≈ ≈ ≈ ≈ ≈ ≈ ≈ ≈ ≈ ≈ ≈ ≈ ≈ ≈ ≈
≈ ≈ ≈ ≈ ≈ ≈ ≈ ≈ ≈ ≈ ≈ ≈ ≈ ≈ ≈ ≈
≈ ≈ ≈ ≈ ≈ ≈ ≈ ≈ ≈ ≈ ≈ ≈ ≈ ≈ ≈ ≈
≈ ≈ ≈ ≈ ≈ ≈ ≈ ≈ ≈ ≈ ≈ ≈ ≈ ≈ ≈ ≈
≈ ≈ ≈ ≈ ≈ ≈ ≈ ≈ ≈ ≈ ≈ ≈ ≈ ≈ ≈ ≈
≈ ≈ ≈ ≈ ≈ ≈ ≈ ≈ ≈ ≈ ≈ ≈ ≈ ≈ ≈ ≈
≈ ≈ ≈ ≈ ≈ ≈ ≈ ≈ ≈ ≈ ≈ ≈ ≈ ≈ ≈ ≈
≈ ≈ ≈ ≈ ≈ ≈ ≈ ≈ ≈ ≈ ≈ ≈ ≈ ≈ ≈ ≈
≈ ≈ ≈ ≈ ≈ ≈ ≈ ≈ ≈ ≈ ≈ ≈ ≈ ≈ ≈ ≈
≈ ≈ ≈ ≈ ≈ ≈ ≈ ≈ ≈ ≈ ≈ ≈ ≈ ≈ ≈ ≈
≈ ≈ ≈ ≈ ≈ ≈ ≈ ≈ ≈ ≈ ≈ ≈ ≈ ≈ ≈ ≈
≈ ≈ ≈ ≈ ≈ ≈ ≈ ≈ ≈ ≈ ≈ ≈ ≈ ≈ ≈ ≈